Reed New Zea

Sea and
Shore Birds

of New Zealand

David G. Medway

REED

By the same author
The Reed Field Guide to Common New Zealand Shorebirds

Cover: Royal Spoonbill with Black-backed Gull.
Title page: Bar-tailed Godwit in breeding plumage.

Established in 1907, Reed Publishing (NZ) Ltd
is New Zealand's largest book publisher, with over 300 titles in print.

For details on all these books visit our website:
www.reed.co.nz

Published by Reed Books, a division of Reed Publishing (NZ) Ltd,
39 Rawene Rd, Birkenhead, Auckland 10.
Associated companies, branches and representatives throughout the world.

ISBN 0 7900 0842 4
First published 2002

Edited by Carolyn Lagahetau
Designed by Graeme Leather

Printed in New Zealand

Contents

Introduction

A large proportion of the bird species found regularly in New Zealand, whether as species which breed there or as migrants which breed elsewhere, are inhabitants of the sea and/or shore. An arbitrarily chosen selection of 50 of those species is described and illustrated in this book.

The status of each species is given — whether it is endemic, native, introduced, migratory or vagrant — together with an indication of its relative numbers — whether it is common, relatively common, locally common, uncommon or rare. For present purposes any migratory species that is present in New Zealand every year, even if only in small numbers, is regarded as common.

Each species is described under four headings. Under **Identification** the average length and weight of the species is given with a brief description of its distinguishing plumage and other physical characteristics. The distribution of the species in New Zealand and the types of habitat it occupies are described under **Distribution & Habitat**. Some account is given of behavioural characteristics which will aid identification of the species concerned, and of what it feeds on, under **Behaviour & Food**, and brief details of the period and places of its breeding are given under **Breeding**. A **Glossary** of some of the terms used in the text is also included.

The order in which each species is described and its common and scientific names follows the order and nomenclature of Turbott, E.G. (ed.), *Checklist of the Birds of New Zealand* (3rd edition. Random Century, Auckland, 1990). Other accounts of species described and illustrated in this book can be found in Heather, B. and Robertson, H., *The Field Guide to the Birds of New Zealand* (Revised edition. Viking, Auckland, 2000), and in Medway, D.G., *The Reed Field Guide to Common New Zealand Shorebirds* (Reed, Auckland, 2000).

David G. Medway
New Plymouth
September 2001

Flesh-footed Shearwater/Toanui

1

Puffinus carneipes

Common native

Family: PROCELLARIIDAE

Identification · Length 44 cm, weight 600 g. Large shearwater, entirely chocolate-brown plumage. Long, narrow, pale pinkish bill with distinctive dark tip. Short legs and feet pinkish.

Distribution & Habitat · New Zealand birds migrate to northern Pacific in March–May after breeding. Returns to colonies in late September. In summer is most often seen in inshore waters off both North Island coasts and eastern South Island.

Behaviour & Food · Slow-flapping flight with long glides near sea-surface, banking in higher winds. Usually solitary at sea, but forms feeding flocks and rafts off nesting colonies.

Food mainly squid and fish, probably caught mostly at night. Attracted to offal behind stationary fishing boats where the birds are vulnerable to drowning after being accidentally hooked on baited fishing lines or becoming entangled in nets.

Breeding · New Zealand population estimated at 25,000–50,000 breeding pairs. Burrow-nests November–May, sometimes in large dense colonies, on islands off northeast coast of the North Island and Auckland's west coast, on islands off New Plymouth and in Cook Strait.

Flesh-footed Shearwater showing diagnostic bill coloration.

2   Buller's Shearwater/Rako   Common endemic
Puffinus bulleri   Family: PROCELLARIIDAE

Identification • Length 46 cm, weight 425 g. Large shearwater, greyish-brown upperparts. Dark 'M' across wings, lower back and rump that creates a distinctive upperwing pattern distinguishing it in flight from other shearwaters. White underparts. Long wedge-shaped tail. Long, slender dark-tipped bluish-grey bill. Short legs and feet pinkish.

Distribution & Habitat • Migrates to northern and eastern Pacific in April–May after breeding. Returns to colonies in mid-September. Common and wide-ranging summer resident of coastal New Zealand waters, particularly in the north.

Behaviour & Food • Graceful, gliding flight interspersed with strong wingbeats. Usually found alone or in small flocks at sea. However, feeding aggregations and resting rafts numbering hundreds of birds are often seen off the New Zealand east coast in summer, occasionally flocks of thousands.

Food includes small krill, small fish, salps and jellyfish taken from the sea-surface. Sometimes scavenges scraps from behind fishing boats.

Breeding • World population *c.* 2.5 million birds. Breeds only on Poor Knights Islands off Northland's east coast where it burrow-nests November–May in large, dense colonies.

Identification • Length 33 cm, weight 300 g. Medium-sized shearwater. Upperparts and face greyish-brown. Underparts are white with faintly mottled partial collar. Underwings white with brownish borders and armpits. Bill is long, thin and dark. Short legs and feet flesh-coloured.

Distribution & Habitat • Widely distributed. Common throughout mainland New Zealand coastal waters. Particularly common in the Hauraki Gulf, Bay of Plenty and Cook Strait. Spends spring and summer in inshore waters close to breeding colonies. In autumn and winter ranges over the continental shelf, inshore waters and harbours. In autumn many fledglings migrate to southeastern Australian waters, most returning July–August.

Behaviour & Food • Gregarious at sea. Flocks sometimes up to 20,000 birds when feeding, resting or on passage. Common in coastal waters and larger harbours. Flies low, fast and direct, just above sea-surface, with quick flapping then gliding.

   Food mostly small fish and krill taken mainly by plunging from a short height above sea-surface, swimming slowly with head submerged and then diving.

Breeding • Estimated 100,000+ pairs breed only in New Zealand. Burrow-nests September–February in dense or scattered colonies, often with other seabirds. Found on many islands, some coastal headlands around coastal North Island and in Cook Strait. Has suffered from mammalian predation at some nesting sites.

4 Southern Giant Petrel
Macronectes giganteus

Uncommon natives
Family: PROCELLARIIDAE

5 Northern Giant Petrel
Macronectes halli

Identification · Length 90 cm, weight 4.5 kg. Very large and bulky petrel. *M. halli*: greyish-brown plumage with paler feathers on face, throat and chest. *M. giganteus*: similar plumage but also has a completely white phase except for scattered dark flecks. Both have massive horn-coloured bills with very prominent nostril tubes. However, tip of bill in *halli* is brownish or pinkish-red, in *giganteus* is pale-green. Short legs and feet dark grey. Separation of the species is difficult at sea.

Distribution & Habitat · Ranges widely throughout the southern oceans. Often seen in New Zealand waters, *halli* probably more common than *giganteus* in summer and autumn, *giganteus* probably more common in winter and spring. Can sometimes be seen close inshore, gliding effortlessly behind the crests of incoming waves.

Behaviour & Food · Flies with several flaps followed by a stiff-winged glide. Often solitary at sea, congregates with other species feeding around fishing boats, when they are often noisy, aggressive.

Well known as voracious scavengers and predators feeding on dead birds, marine mammals and offal. Some kill penguins and small seabirds. Food also includes crustaceans, squid and fish taken from sea-surface.

Breeding · Colonial surface-nester August–April on subantarctic islands, *giganteus* also on Antarctic coast. No *giganteus* nest in the New Zealand region, but c.2500 pairs of *halli* nest on Chatham, Antipodes, Auckland and Campbell islands.

Southern Giant
Petrel showing
diagnostic
greenish-tipped
bill.

Northern Giant
Petrel showing
diagnostic
pinkish-tipped
bill.

6   Grey-faced Petrel/Oi

Common native

Pterodroma macroptera gouldi

Family: PROCELLARIIDAE

Identification • Length 41 cm, weight 550 g. Large petrel. Entirely blackish plumage except for a pale grey forehead, chin, throat and sides of face. Short stout black bill. Short legs and feet black.

Distribution & Habitat • New Zealand birds range widely over Tasman Sea and the southwest Pacific. Most commonly seen over coastal waters off northern New Zealand.

Behaviour & Food • Flight strong. Rapid wheeling and swooping in big arcs with much soaring. Over breeding colonies there are frequent aerial chases just on or after dark, usually accompanied by loud calling. At sea, usually seen alone or in small feeding and roosting flocks. Food is mainly squid, but also some fish and crustaceans, caught mostly at night.

Breeding • New Zealand population estimated at *c.* 250,000 breeding pairs. Burrow-nests June–January in scattered colonies on many islands around northern New Zealand, on some mainland cliffs and headlands as far south as Taranaki. Colonies on mainland suffer from mammalian predation.

ABOVE AND FACING PAGE: Grey-faced Petrel at breeding colony.

7 White-faced Storm Petrel/
Takahikare-moana
Pelagodroma marina maoriana

Common native

Family: HYDROBATIDAE

Identification • Length 20 cm, weight 45 g. Distinctively patterned large storm petrel. White face and eyebrow, conspicuous dark stripe through eye. Greyish-brown upperparts, paler rump, dark wingtips, underparts white. Part of long black legs with yellow-webbed feet project well beyond the tip of the slightly forked black tail in flight. Diagnostic head pattern distinguishes it from all other storm petrels.

Distribution & Habitat • Markedly pelagic when not breeding. New Zealand birds migrate to warmer tropical waters of eastern Pacific in May after breeding, return to colonies September–October. Found in New Zealand coastal waters in summer, common in Hauraki Gulf.

Behaviour & Food • Distinctive foraging and feeding flight: glides slowly forward, wings held outstretched horizontally, legs dangling, gently hopping every few seconds using both feet to push off sea-surface. At sea usually feeds alone, may sometimes form quite large feeding flocks.

Does not usually follow vessels but has been known to take offal thrown overboard from small stationary fishing boats. Surface-feeds on a wide variety of krill, various planktonic crustaceans and small fish.

Breeding • Common burrow-nester October–March on many predator-free islands around New Zealand mainland, at Auckland and Chatham islands. Largest colony of *c.* 850,000 breeding pairs at South East Island.

White-faced Storm Petrel eating fish offal.

Blue Penguin/Korora
Eudyptula minor

8

Identification · Length 40 cm, weight 1.1 kg. Smallest penguin. Dense, short flattened feathers. Upperparts and sides of face including eyes are slate-blue, underparts white. Short flippers are slate-blue, variable white trailing edge. Short robust dark-coloured bill. Very short legs and feet flesh-coloured.

Distribution & Habitat · Generally sedentary, often seen in shallow inshore waters such as harbours close to breeding grounds. Sometimes ashore during the day in seaside caves and cavities. Widespread, locally common around coasts of mainland New Zealand, on nearer offshore islands and Chatham Islands. More common on uninhabited islands and in remote parts of mainland coast away from predation (especially by dogs) and human disturbance, which continue to have a detrimental effect on population and breeding success.

Behaviour & Food · Flightless. Walks upright on land with a waddling gait or short hops, flippers being used to maintain balance. Swims low in the water with head and upper back visible. Frequently comes ashore at night, when it is very vocal.

Feeds at sea by diving mostly within a few metres of surface but can dive to considerable depth. Feeds mainly on small squid and small fish.

Breeding · Breeds August–March. Nests on coasts and offshore islands of mainland New Zealand and on Chatham Islands. Usually solitary nesters, occasionally in loose colonies. Found in burrows, seaside caves, holes in rock piles, under coastal vegetation and sometimes under houses beside the sea. Usually nests near the shore, but some nest hundreds of metres inland, well above sea level.

ABOVE: Blue Penguin in coastal cave.

RIGHT: Rare albino Blue Penguin.

Fiordland Crested Penguin/Tawaki
Eudyptes pachyrhynchus

9

Rare endemic
Family: SPHENISCIDAE

Identification · Length 60 cm, weight 4 kg. Large penguin. Dense, short flattened feathers. Upperparts dark bluish-black, sides of face, chin, throat similar. Rest of underparts white. Broad yellow crest drooping at rear, usually several whitish stripes on cheeks. Robust orange bill with no bare skin at base. Very short legs and feet flesh-coloured. Immatures have a thin eyebrow stripe, whitish chin and throat.

Distribution & Habitat · During breeding adults stay close to shore over continental shelf. Disperse after moulting. Adult and immature stragglers recorded around New Zealand coast and subantarctic islands. Detrimentally affected by predation and disturbance, may now be rarest New Zealand penguin.

Behaviour & Food · Flightless. Walks and swims like the Blue Penguin. Adults return to breeding grounds to moult before dispersing in autumn. Immatures often moult away from breeding grounds.

Sometimes seen in small groups at sea feeding on young squid, octopus, krill and small fish.

Breeding · About 2500–3000 pairs breed only in New Zealand, July–December in small colonies of 10 or fewer pairs. Nests under tree roots, among rockfalls, in crevices or caves, under dense coastal bush or scrub on headlands, islets and around fiord entrances, mostly on the remote coastline of South Westland and islands in Fiordland.

Australasian Gannet/Takapu   Common native
Morus serrator   Family: SULIDAE

Identification • Length 89 cm, weight 2.3 kg. Large seabird, stream-lined body. Long narrow wings and a long tapering tail. Adult white with golden-yellow head, most flight feathers and usually only four central tail feathers are black. Bare facial skin, short throat stripe. Heavy conical pale bluish-grey bill with serrated cutting edges. Short legs and feet slate-grey with bluish-yellow lines down legs and on toes. Immature upperparts are greyish-brown spotted white, underparts are white streaked brown and they have a dark bill.

Distribution & Habitat • Adults and some juveniles widely range New Zealand seas during winter, mostly north of Cook Strait. After breeding almost all juveniles and some adults move to eastern and southern Australian coastal waters, most young birds not returning until 3–7 years old.

Behaviour & Food • Flight direct and powerful with flapping and long gliding. Usually solitary at sea, sometimes travels in small groups and flocks may form over shoals of fish.

Feeds primarily over New Zealand continental shelf and inshore waters, also enters harbours and estuaries. Food is mainly small fish and small squid taken by spectacular plunge-diving, often from a considerable height. Frequently sits on sea-surface when not feeding.

Breeding • Breeding population estimated at 46,000 pairs 1980–81 and increasing. Breeding season variable, generally July–January. Ground nester in large dense colonies on many islands, some headlands around the New Zealand coast. There are accessible mainland colonies at Muriwai, Cape Kidnappers and Farewell Spit.

Australasian Gannet nesting colony.

Nesting Australasian Gannets.

Adult Australasian Gannet.

Black Shag/Kawau
Phalacrocorax carbo novaehollandiae

Common native

Family: PHALACROCORACIDAE

Identification • Length 88 cm, weight 2.2 kg. Largest shag in New Zealand. Long neck, stiff wedge-shaped tail, moderately short rounded wings. Entirely black plumage except for a white patch on cheeks and throat. Yellow facial skin, long narrow greyish bill. Short legs and feet black. Breeding adult has noticeable white thigh patch. Immature similar to adult but dull brown overall, no white cheek or throat patch.

Distribution & Habitat • Common throughout New Zealand and Chatham Islands in estuaries, harbours, coastal waters, inland lakes, rivers and streams.

Behaviour & Food • Does not usually allow close approach. Flight strong, direct with alternate wingbeats and gliding with an extended neck. Swims with head tilted up, body low in the water. Holds out wings to dry when perched after feeding. Often roosts in small groups.

Feeds in lakes, pools in rivers, estuaries, tidal inlets and close inshore on coasts by diving from water surface using webbed feet to swim underwater. Generally feeds alone or in small groups, sometimes larger feeding flocks occur where food is abundant. Feeds mainly on small, medium-sized fish swallowed head first, also takes freshwater crayfish, large invertebrates and molluscs.

Breeding • Most nest in small colonies, sometimes with other shags, in trees overhanging or near water, often well away from the coast. Some nest on coastal cliffs or in low vegetation on offshore stacks. Nest usually a large platform built mainly of sticks and twigs. Nesting season variable, most eggs laid June–October. Parents regurgitate food for chicks.

Black Shag drying wings.

12 Pied Shag/Karuhiruhi
Phalacrocorax varius varius

Locally common native

Family: PHALACROCORACIDAE

Identification · Length 81 cm, weight 2 kg. Large, upperparts glossy black, underparts and face from above eyes white but with black thighs. Long slender greyish bill, yellowish-orange facial skin before eyes, blue eye-ring. Short legs and feet black. Immatures have brownish upperparts, underparts are streaked white, mottled brown.

Distribution & Habitat · Moderately common, 5000–10,000 pairs. Widespread but patchy distribution, mostly northern North Island, northern and southern South Island, Stewart Island. Seldom seen on many parts of mainland New Zealand coastline. Generally sedentary, rarely ventures far inland. Some, mainly juveniles, disperse widely.

Behaviour & Food · Mostly feeds alone, forms small flocks where food is abundant. Often roosts in small groups on logs, rocks and in live or dead trees. Food mainly fish taken by diving.

Breeding · Breeding distribution matches normal distribution around mainland New Zealand. Colonial nester in small groups at some freshwater lakes, usually on coast in live or dead trees, occasionally on artificial structures, sometimes with other shags. Most colonies active all year but have egg-laying peaks.

Adult Pied Shag resting.

Little Shag/Kawaupaka

13

Phalacrocorax melanoleucos brevirostris

Common native

Family: PHALACROCORACIDAE

Identification • Length 56 cm, weight 700 g. Smallest shag in New Zealand. Adults have very variable plumage from entirely black except for white face, sides of head, throat (white-throated phase) to black upperparts, white underparts, face, sides of head (pied phase) with wide array of intermediate 'smudgy' phases. Different phases regularly interbreed.

Juveniles either entirely black or pied. Juvenile black birds are like a small Black Shag, adult and juvenile pied birds are like a small Pied Shag but all Little Shags have short stubby bills, yellow in adults and dark in juveniles. Long stiff black tails, short legs and feet black.

Distribution & Habitat • Widespread, 5000–10,000 pairs and probably increasing. Found throughout mainland New Zealand, Stewart Island and nearer offshore islands, especially common in northern North Island. Frequents a wide variety of habitats coastal and inland, including sheltered coastal waters, estuaries, harbours, lakes, farm ponds, rivers and streams.

Behaviour & Food • Much local movement between feeding and roosting and nesting areas. After breeding, disperses widely from colonies. Often feeds solitarily or in small groups, but can form large roosting, feeding flocks. In coastal areas generally feeds close inshore in shallow water. Food taken by diving but varies according to habitat, mainly eats small fish.

Breeding • Nests throughout New Zealand in colonies of various sizes. Has a very long breeding season, July–May, sometimes together with other shags, especially Pied Shags, usually in trees overhanging water at sheltered locations such as lakes, ponds, swamps or inlets.

Little Shags in white-throated phase.

Little Shag in intermediate phase.

14 Spotted Shag/Parekareka
Stictocarbo punctatus punctatus

Locally common endemic

Family: PHALACROCORACIDAE

Identification · Length 70 cm, weight 1.2 kg. Large and slender greyish shag. Adult breeding plumage distinctive: black spots on back and wings, tail and thighs black, broad white stripe from above eyes down sides of neck, conspicuous double crest, green facial skin. Non-breeding adult has obscure whitish stripe on neck, lacks crests, yellow facial skin, paler underparts. Immature browner, lacks distinctive markings. Short legs and feet yellowish.

Distribution & Habitat · Favours marine environments off rocky shores, seldom seen in other coastal habitats. Widespread but patchy distribution, 10,000–15,000 pairs, probably increasing. Locally common only in a few North Island localities but single birds, usually young, occasionally found well outside normal areas. More common and widespread around most of South Island coastline and Stewart Island.

Behaviour & Food · Much local movement between feeding and nesting areas. When not breeding, may form very large feeding, roosting flocks. Flight rapid, direct and low, often in long lines. Food mainly small fish, marine invertebrates taken by diving mostly in deep water.

Breeding · Breeds only in New Zealand. Season variable year to year and in different places. Nests in colonies of varying sizes, normally apart from other shags, usually on coastal cliffs or rocky islets, often changes nest sites. Impressive colonies on cliff ledges around Banks Peninsula.

ABOVE AND BELOW: Immature Spotted Shag.

White-faced Heron
Common native
Ardea novaehollandiae novaehollandiae

Family: ARDEIDAE

Identification • Length 67 cm, weight 550 g. Large heron. Plumage bluish-grey, white face, chin and upper throat. Long pointed black bill, long greenish-yellow legs. Long narrow plumes on back, particularly in breeding plumage. Immatures are like adults but have no plumes, often only throat white.

Distribution & Habitat • Most common, widespread heron in New Zealand. Found throughout lowland areas in a wide variety of habitats including mudflats, estuaries, rocky shores, harbours, lagoons, lake margins, riverbeds, farmland and parks.

Behaviour & Food • Often solitary but will feed in loose groups in such places as rocky coastal pools and damp pasture. Frequently seen perched on fence posts and water troughs on farmland. Flies steadily, often erratically, with regular deep wingbeats.

Food mainly fish, frogs and tadpoles, it slowly stalks through shallows, darting bill to catch prey.

Breeding • Nests in solitary pairs or small groups, June–February, normally high in trees usually on farmland, sometimes well away from water.

White-faced Heron preening.

16 White Heron/Kotuku
Egretta alba modesta

Uncommon native
Family: ARDEIDAE

Identification · Length 92 cm, weight 900 g. Largest all-white heron. Long thin neck that when outstretched is longer than body. Long straight bill, long legs, broad wings. Breeding plumage: bill black, facial skin green, lower legs black, upper yellowish, long plumes on back. Non-breeding plumage: bill yellow, facial skin greenish-yellow, legs black, no plumes.

Distribution & Habitat · Disperses widely throughout New Zealand mainland, especially northwards, when not breeding. Uncommon in shallow freshwater wetlands, estuaries, mangrove creeks, sometimes seen in rocky coastal pools and damp pasture.

Behaviour & Food · Usually solitary. Quietly walks or stands motionless, lunging at prey when it comes within range. Feeds mainly on small fish, frogs, shrimps, aquatic insects, but will also take small mammals and small birds.

Breeding · New Zealand population 100–120 birds, sometimes augmented by irruptions from Australia. Breeds September–January only in reserve near Okarito, Westland in tall swamp vegetation near Royal Spoonbills.

White Heron taking off.

Identification • Length 66 cm, weight 400 g. Large heron. Long-necked, broad-winged, uniform slate-grey plumage. Long straight heavy dirty-yellowish bill, relatively short yellow-green legs. Variable lengths of plumes on nape, foreneck and back when breeding. Young birds more brown.

Distribution & Habitat • Widespread but uncommon throughout mainland New Zealand and adjacent small islands, most frequent in Northland, decreasing southwards. Mainly on rocky coasts, mangrove-filled estuaries and tidal streams, sometimes intertidal mudflats, very seldom any distance inland.

Behaviour & Food • Usually solitary or in pairs, may roost in small flocks. Strong flier, deep slow wingbeats, neck folded back, head tucked in, legs trailing just above water surface.

Feeds mainly on falling and low tides. Feeding stance crouched, body and head horizontal and neck retracted. Jabs at prey. Diet is mainly small fish, also crabs and molluscs.

Breeding • Solitary nester September–March, in shallow coastal caves and crevices, on rock shelves under overhangs, among or on short coastal vegetation often on stacks, on small islands just offshore.

ABOVE:
Reef Heron resting.

RIGHT:
Reef Heron in alert stance.

OPPOSITE:
Reef Heron fishing.

Royal Spoonbill/Kotuku-ngutupapa
Platalea regia
Locally common native

Family: THRESKIORNITHIDAE

Identification • Length 77 cm, weight 1.7 kg. Large heron-like bird. All white, long black flat spoon-shaped bill with wrinkled surface, black legs, black facial skin marked with yellow patch above eyes, red spot in centre of forehead. Long drooping white plumes on back of head, slight yellowish wash across breast in breeding plumage. Young birds do not have yellow patch above eyes, have a smooth bill and small black tips to wings.

Distribution & Habitat • Disperses widely throughout mainland New Zealand when not breeding. Found on tidal mudflats, muddy estuaries, sometimes on margins of freshwater lakes.

Behaviour & Food • Often gregarious, feeding, roosting and flying in small flocks. Feeds by walking slowly forwards in shallow water, characteristically sweeping slightly open bill from side to side under water. Relies on touch rather than sight to detect food, which is mainly small invertebrates and fish taken at night and by day.

Breeding • First New Zealand breeding record 1949, population now *c.* 700 and increasing by successful breeding at several new colonies. Colonial nester September–February at various localities mainly in the South Island. Near Okarito in Westland in tall trees near White Herons, elsewhere on the ground near Black-backed Gull colonies, or on top of low-growing shrubs near shag colonies.

Royal Spoonbill feeding.

Royal Spoonbill with Black-backed Gull.

Black Swan
Cygnus atratus

Identification • Length 120 cm, weight 6 kg. Unmistakeable. Very large swan, long neck, adult plumage all black except for prominent white wingtips in flight, bill crimson with white bar and tip, short legs and feet black. Immature is dark brown with dull red bill.

Distribution & Habitat • Widespread, common throughout mainland New Zealand and Chatham Islands, population estimated 63,000 in 1981. Greatest numbers on large lowland or coastal lakes, lagoons and in some marine habitats such as Kaipara Harbour, Lake Wairarapa, Farewell Spit and Lake Ellesmere, but many also found on some inland lakes as in the Rotorua area and can be present on lakes in urban parks. Often sits on sea-surface close inshore.

Behaviour & Food • Laborious, noisy take-off from water. Runs across the surface with wings striking the water. Flight strong and steady with slow deep wingbeats, neck outstretched. Groups fly in long lines.

Feeds mainly on aquatic vegetation, dabbling at the surface or upending to reach deeper growth, often grazes on lakeside grass or pasture. Enjoys bread given by humans in urban areas.

Breeding • Long, variable breeding season but mainly July–February. Nests both as solitary pairs and colonially, sometimes up to 5000 nests in a colony, usually on land close to a lake or lagoon, often in stands of raupo, on mounds of vegetation in shallow water at lake or lagoon edges.

Mallard
Anas platyrhynchos platyrhynchos

Common introduction

Family: ANATIDAE

Identification • Length 58 cm, weight 1.3 kg. Large duck. Breeding male: dark glossy green head and neck, separated from chestnut breast by thin white ring around lower foreneck, pale grey body darker on back, black rump and undertail, bill yellowish-green. Female streaked and spotted brown, bill brownish-grey. Non-breeding male like female, but has remnants of green on crown and nape, some chestnut wash on breast.

Both sexes have glossy purple-blue speculum bordered front and back with thin black and white bands, short legs and feet orange. Immature like female. Plumage variable because interbreeds with native Grey Duck *Anas superciliosa superciliosa*. Hybrids very common but can be identified by purple-blue speculum, which in Grey Duck is green, and orangish legs and feet which in Grey Duck are dark-coloured.

Distribution & Habitat • Most numerous and widespread duck throughout mainland New Zealand, also on offshore islands, in a wide variety of habitats including lakes, lagoons, streams, artificial farm ponds and ditches, pasture land, coastal lagoons, estuaries, mudflats and urban parks. Often sits on sea-surface close inshore.

Behaviour & Food • Rises nearly vertically from water surface, flies rapidly and directly with fast shallow wingbeats. Feeds mainly on aquatic vegetation which is obtained by dabbling on surface or by upending, sometimes dives shallowly. Also eats aquatic invertebrates. Grazes on pasture, eats cereals, enjoys bread given by humans in urban areas.

Breeding • Nests solitarily, July–January, usually under dense vegetation not far from water. High mortality among young, often taken by eels.

Mallard showing diagnostic speculum colour.

Mallard pair, male on right.

South Island Pied Oystercatcher/Torea

21

Haematopus ostralegus finschi Common native

Family: HAEMATOPODIDAE

Identification • Length 46 cm, weight 550 g. Large, striking black and white wader, especially in flight when black above, conspicuous broad white wingbars, white wedge on lower back and rump, white below. Head, neck, breast, upper back and tail black. Lower back, rump, flanks and belly white. Sharp border on lower breast between black neck, breast and white belly. White recess on shoulder obvious when standing. Orange eye-ring, scarlet iris. Long, robust, pointed orange-red bill. Short coral-pink legs. Immatures have brownish upperparts, duller bills and legs.

Distribution & Habitat • Spectacular increase in recent decades, estimated 113,000 by 1994. Migrates within New Zealand after breeding. In winter is widely distributed throughout New Zealand, mainly at mudflats, estuaries, beaches; most North Island birds then at Manukau Harbour, Kaipara Harbour, Firth of Thames, most South Island birds in the Nelson area. Departs for breeding grounds late July–September.

Behaviour & Food • Flies fast and direct. Forms huge roosting and feeding flocks of several thousand at wintering locations, often with other species. Feeds at mudflats, estuaries, sandy shores, pastures, ploughed paddocks, riverbeds, by surface picking and deep probing. Eats mainly molluscs, estuarine worms, earthworms and insect larvae.

Breeding • Nests inland, August–January, mostly on shingle riverbeds and farmland, nearly all in eastern South Island. Established pairs usually reclaim same nesting territory although apparently winter at different localities.

Pied Oystercatcher showing white 'mirror' in front of folded wing.

22 Variable Oystercatcher/Torea, Toreapango
Relatively common endemic
Haematopus unicolor Family: HAEMATOPODIDAE

Identification • Length 48 cm, weight 725 g. Large wader. Plumage varies from pied to black with continuous gradient between. Pied phase birds are like South Island Pied Oystercatcher but have band of mottled feathers between black and white plumage of breast, usually no obvious white recess on shoulder. Lower back black or smudgy, not white. Black phase birds all black. Relative abundance of black birds varies with latitude, increasing from north to south. Long, robust somewhat blunted bright-orange bill, short stubby coral-pink legs, orange eye-ring, scarlet iris. Immatures have brownish upperparts, duller bills and legs.

Distribution & Habitat • Population about 4000, widely distributed at estuaries, sandy shores and rocky coastlines. In North Island most common along northeastern coast from North Cape to Mahia Peninsula, and near Wellington. In South Island common around Tasman and Golden bays, Marlborough Sounds, Fiordland, common on beaches of Stewart Island and its offshore islands.

Behaviour & Food • Some occupy breeding territories all year, others gather at estuaries in autumn and winter. May form small winter flocks, sometimes with a few South Island Pied Oystercatchers. Occasionally individual Variable Oystercatchers may be seen among large flocks of that species.

Feeds mostly at estuaries, sandy shores and rock pools, mainly on molluscs, worms, crabs, other small invertebrates and small fish by surface picking and deep probing. Sometimes feeds on earthworms and insect larvae in coastal fields after heavy rain.

Breeding • Pairs, often of different-coloured birds, nest solitarily, September–February, on low flat sites with little or no vegetation such as sandspits, sandy beaches, low sand-dunes, shellbanks, stream mouths on North and South islands, Stewart Island and its offshore islands. Nest sites, particularly on dune areas and beaches, are adversely affected by many factors including mammalian predation and human disturbance.

ABOVE AND RIGHT:
Black phase
Variable
Oystercatcher.

BELOW:
Pied phase
Variable
Oystercatcher.

Australasian Pied Stilt/Poaka Common native
Himantopus himantopus leucocephalus
Family: RECURVIROSTRIDAE

Identification • Length 35 cm, weight 190 g. Distinctive black and white wader. Very long pinkish-red legs, long thin black bill. Head white, hind neck black, in some a black collar encircles lower neck. Back, upper and undersides of wings black, underparts and upper tail white. Immatures have a variable amount of grey on crown, sometimes including eyes, no black hind neck.

Distribution & Habitat • Population recently estimated at 30,000. Widely distributed, common throughout most of lowland North and South islands in suitable wetland habitat such as harbours, estuaries, coastal lakes, shallow lagoons, ponds, swamps and riverbeds. Many South Island and southern North Island birds that nest inland migrate to northern parts of North Island after breeding. Favoured winter localities are Kaipara and Manukau harbours, Firth of Thames, Lake Wairarapa and Lake Ellesmere.

Behaviour & Feeding • Forms flocks at estuaries and lakes outside breeding season where roosts together often in large, compact groups. Nervous and excitable, yapping persistently, noisily when feeding, flying both during day and at night. Feeds in a variety of wetland habitats, including wet pasture. In shallow water pecks at surface or plunges head underneath. Feeds mainly on water insects, also takes small molluscs, crustaceans and earthworms.

Breeding • Nests July–January in loose colonies of up to 20 pairs, sometimes many more, close to water both coastal and inland, on open areas of lake margins, swamps, lagoons, damp fields, gravel riverbeds, estuaries and saltmarshes.

Adult Australasian Pied Stilt.

24 Northern New Zealand Dotterel/ Tuturiwhatu
Uncommon endemic
Charadrius obscurus aquilonius

Family: CHARADRIIDAE

Identification • Length 25 cm, weight 160 g. Stocky plover. Large head, large dark eyes, robust black bill that is slightly upturned at the tip. Breeding plumage: upperparts brown, finely streaked dark brown, white feather edges. Male's breast and belly are red, varying in extent and intensity, females paler. Some breeding pairs show very little reddish coloration. White forehead, pale superciliary streak, olive-grey legs. Sexes similar in non-breeding plumage, no reddish coloration on underparts.

Distribution & Habitat • Threatened endemic subspecies, estimated population 1400. Generally restricted to beaches, rivermouths and estuaries of northern North Island, from North Cape to near Kawhia Harbour in west and to Mahia Peninsula in east. Individual birds occasionally recorded at other North Island localities, particularly on west coast south of normal breeding range. Many flock at favoured coastal sites after breeding, particularly Mangawhai and Omaha on Auckland's east coast, Big Sand Island and Papakanui Spit in Kaipara Harbour.

Behaviour & Food • Often quite confiding and approachable, particularly when roosting in post-breeding flocks. Very territorial during breeding season, usually strenuously defends nest and chicks by employing a wide variety of diversionary tactics.

Feeds mostly on crustaceans, small molluscs, marine organisms including small fish, various sorts of insects obtained mostly along upper tidal levels of foreshore where sandy or stony, at stream mouths, on sandy beaches and dunes, short turf of seaside pastures and sometimes in rock pools.

Breeding • Protracted breeding season, August–February. Virtually whole population nests within its area of general distribution on low flat sites with little or no vegetation, such as sandspits, sandy beaches, low sand dunes, shellbanks and stream mouths. Nest sites, particularly on dune areas and beaches, are adversely affected by many factors including mammalian predation and human disturbance.

Identification • Length 20 cm, weight 60 g. Small plump plover. Upright stance. Confusing array of plumages according to age, sex and season but is the only plover in New Zealand with two breast bands. Breeding plumage: upperparts brown, underparts white except for a thin band on lower neck, brown in females and blackish in males. Both sexes have broader chestnut-coloured breast band. Forehead white, male edged black above. Short dark grey bill and greenish-yellow legs. Non-breeding plumage: male loses black on forehead, in both sexes the breast band fades and is often lost, neck band becomes indistinct.

Distribution & Habitat • Estimated 50,000, most in South Island, but from December to July flocks of up to several hundred are distributed around the New Zealand coast in a wide range of habitats including estuaries, sandy beaches, stream mouths, coastal lakes and ponds, salt-marshes, coastal farmland, ploughed fields and airports. Complex, regionally specific post-breeding movements, including migration of large numbers from particular South Island populations to wintering areas in southeastern Australia.

Behaviour & Food • Feeds in loose flocks or alone, running, walking and randomly stopping to peck and probe. Relies principally on invertebrates of aquatic and near-aquatic sources.

Breeding • Nests throughout New Zealand, July–January. Wide range of habitats including inland riverbeds and lakeshores, subalpine herbfields, rivermouths, beaches, coastal lagoons and pastures. Nests are vulnerable to flooding, mammalian predation and human disturbance. Some feeding and breeding riverbed habitats have been seriously degraded by encroachment of introduced plants.

Juvenile Banded Dotterel.

Shore Plover/Tuturuatu
Thinornis novaeseelandiae

Rare endemic

Family: CHARADRIIDAE

Identification • Length 20 cm, weight 60 g. Distinctive small and stocky dotterel. Crown and upperparts greyish-brown, forehead, sides of face and throat black in males, dark brown in females. White ring around back of head above eyes across forehead, underparts white. Red black-tipped bill and short orange legs.

Distribution & Habitat • Endangered endemic species. Only about 150 survive naturally on predator-free South East Island and Western Reef near Chatham Island, rarely wandering to other nearby islands. Captive-bred birds recently released on Motuora Island in Hauraki Gulf and Portland Island in Hawke Bay. Neither population is yet self-sustaining. Birds from those islands are quite regularly seen on nearby North Island estuaries, others have wandered more widely. In its natural habitat lives on coastal rocky wave platforms and on exposed saltmeadow. Has been seen on rocky coastline and estuarine habitats on mainland.

Behaviour & Food • Strongly territorial in breeding season. In winter may roost and feed in small flocks. Birds seen on North Island mainland usually solitary. Gleans and pecks among tide-wrack, on wet rock platforms, in rocky tidal pools with algae and barnacles. Food includes crustaceans, molluscs, spiders, insects and their larvae.

Breeding • Naturally, October–February, in nests hidden under thick vegetation, sometimes under boulders near the shore or under large rocks inland. Very vulnerable to mammalian predation. No doubt this is the reason it survives naturally only on predator-free islands.

Wrybill/Ngutuparore
Anarhynchus frontalis

Locally common endemic
Family: CHARADRIIDAE

Identification · Length 20 cm, weight 55 g. Distinctive, small grey and white plover with short grey-green legs. Long narrow black bill is unique in that the last third of it turns to the right. Males and females are reliably distinguished only in breeding plumage. Crown, nape, upperparts plain ashy-grey, white forehead in male edged with thin black frontal band. Underparts white, black band across upper breast is wider in male. In non-breeding plumage males have no black frontal band, in both sexes the breast band is indistinct or absent.

Distribution & Habitat · Threatened endemic species. World population not more than 5000, evidence that this is decreasing. Begins arriving at principal wintering grounds in harbours of Northland, Auckland and South Auckland during late December–January. In winter, almost all are in North Island, notably at Firth of Thames and Manukau Harbour. Departs for South Island breeding grounds from late July.

Behaviour & Food · Roosts quietly in dense flocks, usually apart from other waders, but some other small species often found resting among them. Confiding and approachable when at rest. Large numbers often perform swift and spectacular aerial displays, particularly before southward migration.

Opportunistic feeders, relying mainly on invertebrates of aquatic and near-aquatic sources. Commonly feeds by pecking insects off the water's surface, or by tilting its head to left followed by clockwise movements of bill under stones in shallow pools. Feeds mostly on mayfly larvae, bugs, beetles, flies at nesting grounds and small crustaceans on tidal mudflats of wintering grounds.

Breeding · Nests August–January, only on braided riverbeds in Canterbury and inland Otago, usually on islands of bare shingle, or on a high point without vegetation on a shingle bank near water. Nests vulnerable to flooding, mammalian predation and human disturbance. Some feeding and breeding riverbed habitats have been seriously degraded by encroachment of introduced plants.

RIGHT:
Female Wrybill in breeding plumage.

BELOW:
Male Wrybill in breeding plumage.

Pacific Golden Plover
Pluvialis fulva

Common Arctic migrant
Family: CHARADRIIDAE

Identification • Length 25 cm, weight 130 g. Medium-sized plover. Non-breeding plumage: upperparts mottled brown and buff with golden suffusion, throat and breast grey and yellowish-buff. Breeding plumage: striking, white forehead, upperparts brownish, heavily speckled golden yellow and white, black face and underparts separated from upperparts by a broad white stripe from above eyes down sides of body to flanks. Large black eyes, short black bill and long, generally dark grey legs.

Distribution & Habitat • Fourth most numerous Arctic wader to visit New Zealand each year. Arrives from September, estimated 650 every summer but numbers vary widely from year to year. Widespread at a number of harbours, estuaries and some lakes throughout New Zealand. Favoured localities are Parengarenga, Kaipara and Manukau harbours, Lake Wairarapa in North Island and Lake Ellesmere and Invercargill Estuary in South Island. Most depart late March–early April, very seldom winters in New Zealand.

Behaviour & Food • Generally found in small loose flocks, which may be on a beach or mudflat one day, on short pasture or ploughed land the next. Does not form compact groups when roosting, usually somewhat scattered, often not using the same roosts as other waders. Normally alert and shy, difficult to approach closely. Flies swiftly and directly in groups with strong and regular wingbeats.

Feeds on a wide range of insects and their larvae, spiders, earthworms, plant seeds, small crustaceans, molluscs and marine worms.

Breeding • Nests on Arctic and subarctic tundra of Siberia and western Alaska during the northern summer. Migrates widely after breeding including to Australasia and most Pacific islands.

Pacific Golden Plovers and Terek Sandpiper.

Pacific Golden Plover moulting.

Pacific Golden Plover in breeding plumage.

Spur-winged Plover

Common native

Vanellus miles novaehollandiae

Family: CHARADRIIDAE

Identification • Conspicuous large plover. Broad-winged, strikingly patterned, unlike any other bird in New Zealand. Adult: black crown and hindneck, broad black stripe on each side of body from hindneck to sides of breast, brown back. Brown and black upperwing distinctive in flight. Rump white, upper tail white, conspicuous black band near tip. Underwings white, broad dark trailing edge conspicuous in flight. Yellow bill, large bright yellow wattles, long reddish legs, long sharp spur on wings. Young: duller, mottled upperparts and upperwings.

Distribution & Habitat • Extensive open pastures and arable farmlands in New Zealand provide much suitable habitat. Occurs throughout New Zealand, numbers not known but probably tens of thousands and increasing, in a wide variety of habitats including farmlands, wetlands, estuaries, rocky and sandy coasts. Can be a serious hazard at airports.

Behaviour & Food • Flies buoyantly, slow with deliberate beats of rounded wings. Has an unmistakeable penetrating call given by day, sometimes at night. Very wary, alert. Has a variety of distraction displays, is aggressive, particularly in defence of nest and chicks. Often gregarious when not breeding, sometimes forming large flocks. Feeds with slow stalking walk, shoulders hunched and head forward, on earthworms, insects and their larvae, seeds, leaves, crustaceans and molluscs.

Breeding • Long breeding season, June–December. Nests in variety of grassland and shingle riverbed habitats, preferred sites are rough open pasture, bare ground with wide outlook.

Spur-winged Plover in aggressive mood showing spurs on wings.

Adult Spur-winged Plover incubating.

30

Turnstone
Arenaria interpres

Common Arctic migrant
Family: CHARADRIIDAE

Identification • Length 23 cm, weight 120 g. Medium-sized wader. Easily distinguished from other similar-sized waders by stout shape, contrasting black, white and chestnut plumage, short wedge-shaped black bill, short orange legs. In flight distinguished by dark upperparts contrasting with white wingbars, white lower back and white band on upper tail. Sexes different in breeding plumage. Males: black and white patterning over face and breast, variable white cap, nape finely streaked black, rich chestnut and black variegated back and wings, and white abdomen. Females: duller, brown wash over much of head, less distinct black and white patterning. Non-breeding plumage: duller, head and upperparts dark brown, mottled black and chestnut, face variegated white, black and brown, broad blackish band on upper breast, rest of underparts white. Juveniles have dusky heads, duller coloration.

Distribution & Habitat • Third most numerous Arctic wader to visit New Zealand each year. Arrives from late August, estimated 5000 every summer but numbers vary quite widely from year to year. Widespread, more or less evenly distributed between both main islands although rarely on western coast of South Island. Concentrates in certain favoured coastal localities, mainly northern harbours, Nelson–Marlborough region and southern estuaries. Most depart March–April, a few hundred winter in New Zealand.

Behaviour & Food • Gregarious. Forms flocks of various sizes, often roosts near to but apart from other resting birds. Tends to avoid smooth sandy beaches, open mudflats and sandflats, prefers feeding among rock pools, on exposed rocky reefs, shelly or stony foreshores. Picks and probes at stranded debris in search of food. Dashes quickly between waves, pecking and searching. Feeds on sandhoppers, mud crabs and molluscs.

Breeding • Nests along northern coasts and islands of Greenland, Scandinavia, Siberia, Alaska and islands of northern Canada during northern summer, almost cosmopolitan after breeding.

Female Turnstone in breeding plumage.

31

Lesser Knot/Huahou
Calidris canutus rogersi

Common Arctic migrant
Family: SCOLOPACIDAE

Identification · Length 24 cm, weight 120 g. Medium-sized robust wader. Short straight black bill, short dull-green legs. Non-breeding plumage: plain grey upperparts, paler feather edges, underparts pale-grey to off-white. Light grey speckling on neck, breast and flanks. Pale rump barred white and grey, indistinct white wingbar shows in flight. Breeding plumage: females less resplendent than males, head, neck and breast rusty-red, back black with rusty, white speckling. Juveniles are generally like non-breeding adults.

Distribution & Habitat · Second most numerous Arctic wader to visit New Zealand each year. Arrives from late August, estimated 59,000 every summer but numbers vary quite widely year to year. Widespread but favour only a few localities, being several northern harbours, most notably Manukau Harbour, and Farewell Spit at the top of the South Island. Main flocks depart March–April, a few thousand winter in New Zealand mostly at Manukau Harbour.

Behaviour & Food · Very gregarious, flies, feeds and roosts in large numbers, sometimes roosts apart from other waders, but commonly associates with Bar-tailed Godwits with which forms impressive roosting flocks, often numbering many thousands, usually on sandbanks, shell-banks, spits, sometimes on dry mud pans and on coastal lagoon edges.

Usually feeds on intertidal mudflats, sandflats, sometimes on saltmarshes and on coastal pastures where vegetation is short and the ground wet. Feeds on falling tide with 'sewing machine' action, rapidly drilling soft mud and wet sand. Head is held low and the bill is nearly vertical. Feeds mainly on small molluscs, crustaceans, marine worms and insects.

Breeding · Nests in extreme high Arctic during northern summer, migrates after breeding to as far south as South Africa, Australasia and southern South America. Australasian birds breed on the Chukotski Peninsula in eastern Siberia.

Lesser Knot in non-breeding plumage.

32

Curlew Sandpiper
Calidris ferruginea

Common Arctic migrant
Family: SCOLOPACIDAE

Identification · Length 19 cm, weight 60 g. Small slim wader. Long thin down-curved black bill, longish black legs, white rump and narrow white wingbar that is conspicuous in flight. Non-breeding plumage: pale grey-brown head and upperparts, white superciliary stripes, white underparts with pale grey wash, dark streaks on breast. Brilliant in breeding plumage, males particularly so with rich rufous on breast and sides of head, upperparts dark to reddish-brown, whitish edges to dark-centred feathers giving spangled effect. Crown has a rich, waved lateral pattern. There are touches of white on the sides, on the edges of the dark brown wing feathers, and on the upper tail coverts, which are barred with black. Juveniles are like non-breeding adults but neck and breast washed buff.

Distribution & Habitat · Seventh most numerous Arctic wader to visit New Zealand each year. Arrives from early September and is among first of the arctic waders to do so. The estimated 85 every summer are widespread, larger flocks exceptional, small numbers regularly reported from many harbours and estuaries, most consistently present each year in largest numbers at Lake Ellesmere. Some stay long after other Arctic waders have departed, very few normally winter in New Zealand.

Behaviour & Food · Groups particularly spectacular in flight, very swift with high chattering calls, twisting and turning sharply in all directions. Favours tidal flats, brackish pools, margins of some coastal lakes and lagoons. Roosts and feeds mainly with Wrybills where they are present, and with Banded Dotterels and Lesser Knots. One or two in non-breeding plumage are very difficult to detect when they are roosting among large groups of Lesser Knots.

Feeds on marine worms, molluscs and crustaceans that it obtains in bare wet mud, shallow water, by picking from the surface and probing deeply with long bill.

Breeding · Nests in high Arctic central Siberia during the northern summer, a few have bred in Alaska well to the east of normal range. Migrates after breeding to Africa, southern Asia and Australasia.

Curlew Sandpiper in non-breeding plumage.

Curlew Sandpipers feeding with Lesser Knot.

Curlew Sandpiper in breeding plumage.

33 Sharp-tailed Sandpiper
Calidris acuminata

Common Arctic migrant

Family: SCOLOPACIDAE

Identification · Length 22 cm, weight 60 g. Medium-sized brownish wader. Shortish dark bill and yellowish-green legs. Individuals vary considerably in appearance with age and season. Non-breeding adults: rufous crown streaked black, whitish superciliary stripes. Upperparts dark brown, pale feather edges, rump and tail dark brown, white sides. Neck and breast mottled grey, usually with irregular dark streaks, breast fades to white on abdomen. Breeding plumage: upperparts rich chestnut with buff feather edges, neck and breast heavily streaked, small dark crescentic streaks develop on lower breast and flanks. Juveniles: broad superciliary stripes, very distinct bright rufous cap, foreneck and upper breast orange-buff, narrow gorget of fine streaks across upper neck.

Distribution & Habitat · Eighth most numerous Arctic wader to visit New Zealand each year. Arrives from late September, estimated about 80 every summer but numbers vary quite widely year to year. Widespread at estuaries and lakes with average numbers being highest at Firth of Thames, Lake Ellesmere and Invercargill Estuary. Small numbers regularly frequent some other suitable localities. Departs March–April, seldom winters in New Zealand.

Behaviour & Food · Often found in small flocks, tend to keep to themselves but on tidal mudflats may associate with Lesser Knots, Curlew Sandpipers and Red-necked Stints. Frequently roosts apart from other birds, sometimes with other small waders, such as Wrybills, on shellbanks and sandbanks.

Feeds on tidal mudflats well back from the tideline, prefers coastal lakes, lagoons and pools where it often feeds and roosts around edges, sometimes hidden among vegetation. Feeds on molluscs, crustaceans, worms, insects and seeds.

Breeding · Nests in northeastern Siberia during northern summer, migrates after breeding to New Guinea, Australasia, some also reaching Vanuatu, New Caledonia and Fiji.

Sharp-tailed Sandpiper in breeding plumage.

Sharp-tailed Sandpipers in non-breeding plumage.

Red-necked Stint
Calidris ruficollis

Common Arctic migrant
Family: SCOLOPACIDAE

Identification • Length 15 cm, weight 30 g. Smallest Arctic wader to regularly visit New Zealand. Short stubby black bill, short black legs. Non-breeding plumage: predominantly grey and white. Crown, sides of face, hindneck and upperparts are pale grey, brownish tinge. Chin, throat and belly white, breast has variable amounts grey flecking. Breeding plumage: sides of face, chin, throat, neck brick-red, rest of underparts white, some dusky flecking on sides of breast. Crown and back blackish-brown with rufous margins. Juveniles are like non-breeding adults but crown and sides of breast are washed pale rufous, back feathers are dark rufous-edged.

Distribution & Habitat • Fifth most numerous Arctic wader to visit New Zealand each year. Arrives from late September, estimated about 175 every summer. Lake Ellesmere most favoured locality, Awarua Bay, Manukau Harbour and Farewell Spit also important, a few at other suitable places each year. Departs from late March, several spend the winter in New Zealand.

Behaviour & Food • Swift, agile flier. Usually associates with other small waders and can often be found among flocks of wintering Wrybills at high-tide roosts.

Voracious feeder, mainly at tidal mudflats, sandflats, saltmarshes and margins of coastal lagoons, where it busily runs about probing and pecking with rapid 'sewing-machine' action. Virtually nothing known about food in New Zealand, in Australia mostly small marine invertebrates, molluscs, crustaceans and insects.

Breeding • Nests in northern Siberia and northwestern Alaska during northern summer, migrates after breeding to Malaysia, Philippines and Australasia, especially southeastern Australia.

35 Eastern Broad-billed Sandpiper
Limicola falcinellus sibiricus   Rare Arctic vagrant
Family: SCOLOPACIDAE

Identification • Length 17 cm, weight 35 g. Small pale wader, smaller than Wrybill, marginally larger than Red-necked Stint. Long broad blackish bill downturned at tip, short olive-green legs. Non-breeding: upperparts pale grey-brown with dark centres to some larger feathers, double white supercilium. Underparts white, breast lightly streaked grey-brown. Breeding plumage: upperparts darker, feathers thinly edged buff and rufous, giving a streaked appearance. Heavily streaked breast divided neatly from white belly. Juvenile similar to breeding adult. Double supercilium in all plumages and long broad downturned bill are sure pointers to identity.

Distribution & Habitat • Rare visitor to New Zealand, may sometimes be overlooked because associates, particularly when roosting, with other small, superficially similar-looking species such as Wrybills, Red-necked Stints and Curlew Sandpipers. First recorded at Firth of Thames in 1960. Most sightings are of single birds, occasionally two together. Almost all confirmed records are from the North Island, only confirmed South Island record was a single bird at Lake Ellesmere.

Behaviour & Food • Walks quickly, sometimes runs. Feeds at soft intertidal mudflats and coastal lake margins, probing vigorously up and down, occasionally pecking at surface. Food in New Zealand not known, overseas is mainly worms, molluscs, crustaceans, insects and seeds.

Breeding • Birds visiting New Zealand nest in eastern Siberia during northern summer, migrate after breeding mainly to southeastern Asia and northwestern Australia.

Family: SCOLOPACIDAE

Identification • Length 63 cm, weight 900 g. Largest wader visiting New Zealand. Spectacular bird with a distinctive very long, downcurved bill. Entire body is streaked greyish-brown, paler on underparts, indistinct pale superciliary stripe, brown rump. Bill dark brown, pink base to lower mandible, bluish-grey legs. The combination of large size, long down-curved bill and uniformly patterned plumage readily distinguishes it from all other waders in New Zealand.

Distribution & Habitat • Ninth most numerous Arctic wader to visit New Zealand each year. Arrives from late September, estimated about 35 every summer, may be decreasing. Found at localities most frequented by other waders. Although widespread during summer, most reported from only three sites: Manukau Harbour, Firth of Thames, and Farewell Spit which has always been a favoured locality. Departs from late March, but a high proportion spend winter in New Zealand.

Behaviour & Food • Associates with Bar-tailed Godwits, Lesser Knots and South Island Pied Oystercatchers at high-tide roosts, but tends to keep slightly apart from other waders so is easily noticed. Very wary, difficult to approach when both feeding and roosting, easily put to flight. Solitary birds sometimes chased from high-tide roosts by Bar-tailed Godwits, which hotly pursue the calling curlew.

Feeds mainly in tidal estuaries, harbours but also in muddy coastal lagoons, mostly on crustaceans and marine worms obtained by probing deeply into mud and picking at surface.

Breeding • Nests in northeastern Asia during northern summer, migrates after breeding to Australasia, particularly to northern and eastern Australia.

37

Whimbrel
Numenius phaeopus

Common Arctic migrant
Family: SCOLOPACIDAE

Identification · Length 43 cm, weight 450 g. Large wader, about the same size as the Bar-tailed Godwit, but looks darker, more robust. Has long distinctly downcurved black bill. Almost completely streaked brown and buff, crown dark brown with clear pale stripe down centre that is very distinctive when seen from front. Bluish-grey legs. Two subspecies occur in New Zealand, Asiatic and American, and they are normally indistinguishable on the ground. Asiatic, the subspecies more commonly found in Australasia, has whitish barred brown lower back and rump in contrast to uniform brown of the rest of its upperparts. American has brown lower back, rump uniform in coloration with rest of upperparts. Not safe to identify a Whimbrel to subspecies unless this feature is clearly seen, normally only in flight.

Distribution & Habitat · Sixth most numerous Arctic wader to visit New Zealand each year. Arrives from late September, estimated about 120 every summer but numbers vary widely year to year. Found in tidal estuaries and harbours, the most favoured sites being Parengarenga and Kaipara harbours, Firth of Thames, Farewell Spit. Departs from late March, but a high proportion spend winter in New Zealand.

Behaviour & Food · Gregarious. Individuals of both subspecies sometimes associate temporarily. A single roosting bird is almost impossible to find among Bar-tailed Godwits until it lifts its head and shows its downcurved bill. Usually feeds and roosts in small groups, often very wary, standing alert at the edge of other roosting waders. Does not allow close approach. Feeds mainly on crabs, marine worms picked from surface and taken by probing.

Breeding · Asiatic Whimbrel nests in eastern Siberia, American Whimbrel in northern North America during northern summer.

38

Eastern Bar-tailed Godwit/Kuaka
Limosa lapponica baueri Common Arctic migrant
Family: SCOLOPACIDAE

Identification • Length 40 cm, weight 325 g. Large wader whose colour, proportions, long legs and long slightly upturned bill readily distinguish it from other birds with which it commonly associates in New Zealand. Females are distinctly larger than males, difference especially noticeable in bill length. Bill black with pink base, legs black. Non-breeding plumage: upperparts mottled brown and grey, lower back rump and tail barred white and brown, underparts dull-white, clouded grey. Striking in full breeding plumage. Male's upperparts are patterned black and buff, face, neck and underparts are brick-red, female's buffy red with fine barring. Juveniles are like non-breeding adults, but more buff and they have more distinctly mottled upperparts.

Distribution & Habitat • Most numerous Arctic wader to visit New Zealand each year. Arrives from mid-September, estimated 102,000 every summer but numbers vary quite widely year to year. Found throughout New Zealand at harbours, estuaries, sandy coasts, particularly at inlets, estuaries with broad intertidal mudflats and sandflats. Most abundant at Manukau and Kaipara harbours and Farewell Spit, but some other northern harbours have several thousand every summer. Main flocks depart March–April, several thousand winter in New Zealand with the majority at Manukau and Kaipara harbours and Farewell Spit.

Behaviour & Feeding • Very gregarious, feeds in loose groups, roosts in flocks which may number thousands, often in the company of Lesser Knots. Found on sandbanks, shellbanks, spits, also saltmarshes, shallow coastal lagoon edges and coastal paddocks. Flies swiftly, often in compact groups, with much twisting and turning in unison or directly in long lines, V-formation. Spectacular as flight after flight comes in to high-tide roosts. Feeds on falling tideline, obtaining mainly marine worms, molluscs and crabs from surface with rapid stabs of bill, or deep in mud and sand by probing.

Breeding • Nests in eastern Siberia, northern Alaska during northern summer, migrates after breeding to southeast Asia and Australasia.

Bar-tailed Godwit in breeding plumage.

Bar-tailed Godwits in non-breeding plumage.

39

Wandering Tattler
Tringa incana

Uncommon Arctic migrant
Family: SCOLOPACIDAE

Identification · Length 27 cm, weight 120 g. Medium-sized wader. Long wings and tail give attenuated rear-end. Long straight dark grey bill, very long nasal groove diagnostic at close quarters. Short yellowish legs. Non-breeding plumage: upperparts, breast and flanks plain slate grey, rest of underparts white, whitish supercilium prominent only in front of eye. Breeding plumage: all underparts except for a small area on belly and vent are heavily barred dark grey. Juveniles similar to non-breeding adult but have fine grey barring on breast and flanks.

Distribution & Habitat · Uncommon, possibly annual visitor to New Zealand. Prefers rocky coasts and reefs to tidal mudflats, estuaries and beaches.

Behaviour & Food · Usually wary and solitary, sometimes feeds in small groups. Flies fast, usually low and direct, with flicking beats. Flight call diagnostic rippling trill of 6–10 notes. Bobs and teeters almost continuously when feeding, mostly on marine worms, molluscs and crustaceans.

Breeding · Nests in eastern Siberia and northwest North America during northern summer. Migrates after breeding to American coast from California to Peru and many South Pacific islands, some as far as New Zealand and eastern Australia.

Wandering Tattler showing diagnostic long nasal groove.

40

Siberian Tattler   Uncommon Arctic migrant
Tringa brevipes   Family: SCOLOPACIDAE

Identification • Length 25 cm, weight 100 g. Very similar to Wandering Tattler but slightly smaller, nasal groove much shorter, plumage usually a little paler. White supercilium extends beyond eye. Breeding plumage: belly and undertail remain white, not generally barred as in Wandering Tattler. Juveniles are similar to non-breeding adults but have fine grey barring on breast and flanks.

Distribution & Habitat • Uncommon, a few probably reach New Zealand every year. Quite regularly recorded in suitable habitats. Prefers tidal mudflats, sometimes seen on rocky coasts.

Behaviour & Food • Usually wary and solitary, sometimes feeds in small groups. Flies fast, usually low and direct, with flicking beats. Flight call diagnostic high-pitched two-syllables, unlike rippling trill of Wandering Tattler. Bobs and teeters almost continuously when feeding. Feeds mostly on marine worms, molluscs and crustaceans.

Breeding • Nests patchily across northern Asia in northern summer, migrates after breeding to southeast Asia, Philippines, Australasia and southwest Pacific islands.

Identification • Length 23 cm, weight 70 g. Small wader. Long thin distinctly upcurved black bill that is yellowish at the base, short orange-yellow legs distinguish it from all other small waders. Non-breeding plumage: faint white superciliary stripe, upperparts brownish-grey, underparts white, dark patch at bend of folded wing, faint streaks on neck and breast that vary seasonally in intensity. White-tipped secondaries forming broad white trailing edge to upperwing, pale sides to rump, tail show clearly in flight. Breeding plumage: browner, more flecking, especially on breast. Juveniles generally look like a breeding adult.

Distribution & Habitat • A regular, probably annual, visitor in small numbers. Favours tidal creeks, coastal lagoons and estuarine mudflats. Has been recorded from Northland to Southland lagoons. Firth of Thames and Manawatu Estuary are among favoured localities.

Behaviour & Food • Usually roost among Wrybills, where present, when they can be very difficult to distinguish, especially when sleeping, unless yellowish legs and long upturned bill are seen. Often remains alert and active at high-tide roosts, may be the only bird moving about. Sometimes runs around calling frequently. Bobs head and tail.

Feeds like a dotterel, running quickly in all directions, stopping, pecking at prey, then running here and there again. Pecks at surface and probes deeply. Feeds mostly on crustaceans and insects.

Breeding • Nests from Finland across Siberia in northern summer, migrates widely after breeding including to coasts of south and southeast Asia, Philippines, particularly common in many parts of northern and eastern Australia.

Southern Black-backed Gull/Karoro

42

Larus dominicanus dominicanus

Common native
Family: LARIDAE

Identification · Length 60 cm, weight 950 g. Largest gull in New Zealand. Adult has black back and upperwings with narrow white trailing edge. White head, neck, underparts, rump and tail. Bill yellow and heavy, with a red spot near tip of lower mandible. Greenish-yellow legs and feet. Complicated succession of plumage changes from juvenile to adult, from generally mottled dull brown in juvenile to black and white adult.

Distribution & Habitat · Aggressive, successful species. Most abundant, widespread gull, perhaps *c.* 1,000,000 breeding pairs. Lives in a wide variety of habitats from coastal to alpine areas.

Behaviour & Food · Aggressive and generally gregarious. Frequently feeds and roosts in large groups, commonly associates with Red-billed Gulls. Mainly sedentary, but commutes between roosting sites and feeding areas, rarely ventures far out to sea. Strong flier, 'patrols' with its beak pointed downwards, scans area with sharp, sweeping movements of the head.

Feeds in many habitats including coastal rubbish dumps, on an exceptionally wide range of items such as offal, refuse, carrion, small fish, marine molluscs, worms, beetles, frogs, lizards, scraps given by humans, eggs and chicks of own and some other species.

Breeding · Nests October–February, usually in colonies that are often very large, sometimes as solitary pairs or in small groups. Nests in both coastal and inland areas including on dunes, sandspits, boulder banks, gravel beaches, islands, rocky islets, lakeshores, riverbeds, high mountain-tarns and roofs of city buildings.

Juvenile Black-backed Gull.

43

Red-billed Gull/Tarapunga   Common native
Larus novaehollandiae scopulinus

Family: LARIDAE

Identification · Length 37 cm, weight 280 g. Small, slender, grey and white plumaged gull. Adult readily identified by bright red eye-ring, stoutish bright red bill, bright red legs and feet and distinctive dark-tipped upperwings in flight. Red coloration of bare parts is duller outside the breeding season. Very young birds have upperwing coverts that are heavily spotted brownish. There are confusing and poorly known changes in coloration of the bill and legs with age, season and individual variation.

Distribution & Habitat · Perhaps more than 100,000 breeding pairs, predominantly in coastal areas, more common on coasts of eastern North and South islands. Rarely ventures far inland but is regularly seen at parks, sportsgrounds and flooded bowling greens in coastal cities and towns. Many make regular seasonal movements between breeding colonies and traditional wintering areas.

Behaviour & Food · Aggressive and generally gregarious. Frequently feeds and roosts in large groups, commonly associates with Southern Black-backed Gulls. Mainly sedentary, but commutes between roosting sites and feeding areas, rarely ventures far out to sea.

Feeds in many habitats including coastal rubbish dumps, on an exceptionally wide range of items which can change somewhat with season, such as planktonic crustaceans, small fish, offal, garbage, beetles, sand-hoppers, tadpoles, earthworms, scraps given by humans, eggs of own and some other species and even food robbed from other birds.

Breeding · Nests October–February, almost exclusively on coastline, but there is also an inland colony at Rotorua. Mostly found on sandspits, boulderbanks, shellbanks, gravel beaches, rocky headlands, rocky islands and islets.

INSET: Adult Red-billed Gull in breeding plumage.

44

Black-billed Gull
Larus bulleri

Common endemic
Family: LARIDAE

Identification • Length 37 cm, weight 275 g. Small, slender, grey and white plumaged gull. Adult readily identified by black eye-ring that sometimes has a dark red tinge. Slender longish black bill, normally black legs and feet. Distinctive pale-tipped upperwings in flight. Very young birds have upperwing coverts that are heavily spotted brownish. There are confusing and poorly known changes in coloration of bill and legs with age, season and individual variation.

Distribution & Habitat • About 45,000 breeding pairs, not as widely distributed as Red-billed Gulls. During the breeding season is found mainly in inland eastern South Island on larger rivers, lakes and nearby arable land. Disperses widely after breeding, mostly to coastal areas, some migrating to southern North Island. During winter can be found at estuaries, harbours, lakes, open coastlines, parks of coastal towns, frequently in the company of Red-billed Gulls.

Behaviour & Food • Scavenges less than other New Zealand gulls. During the breeding season feeds mainly on small freshwater fish, invertebrates and insects and larvae. During winter eats a wider variety of food that includes marine and freshwater invertebrates, small fish, worms, insects and scraps fed by humans.

Breeding • Nests September–February, mainly in eastern South Island in large, densely packed colonies on braided riverbeds, sandspits, boulderbanks and shellbanks. In the North Island some nest at Firth of Thames, Manukau and Kaipara harbours and inland at Rotorua. Riverbed nesting habitat has been detrimentally affected by hydroelectric storage lakes, encroachment of introduced plants, mammalian predators and human disturbance.

ABOVE:
Adult Black-billed
Gulls.

RIGHT:
Juvenile Black-
billed Gull.

OPPOSITE:
Immature Black-
billed Gull.

45

White-winged Black Tern
Chlidonias leucopterus Common Asian migrant
Family: LARIDAE

Identification • Length 23 cm, weight 65 g. Small tern with only slightly forked tail. Striking and unmistakeable in breeding plumage: all black except for a white rump and vent area, very pale grey upperwing darker at tips, white tipped underwing, red bill, very short legs and feet red. Non-breeding plumage: generally grey and white, but distinctive black club-shaped band extends over the top of the head from behind the eyes and down nape. Generally has a black bill and legs. Bewildering array of seasonally intermediate plumages, but all have the club-shaped band over head and down nape. Immatures are generally like non-breeding adults. Birds in breeding plumage may be seen at any time of the year.

Distribution & Habitat • Regular annual migrant to New Zealand, appears to be either becoming more common or more frequently reported. Widespread from Northland to Southland at coastal localities such as harbours, estuaries, lakes, lagoons and oxidation ponds. Sometimes several birds seen together at a favoured locality.

Behaviour & Food • Distinctive feeding pattern when hawking insects over water. Flies repeatedly into the wind and back again, generally over the same area, dropping to pick insects from water's surface. Rarely plunges.

Breeding • Nests in marshes across Eurasia, north to Siberia, probably in East Africa in northern summer. Migrates to southern hemisphere after breeding, including to Australasia.

White-winged Black Tern.

White-winged Black Terns in flight.

Identification • Length 29 cm, weight 80 g. Noticeably smaller and greyer than White-fronted Tern, which it often associates with. Always has bright orange legs and feet, irrespective of age and season. Distinctive in breeding plumage. Jet black crown from bill to nape and around eyes. Black crown is separated from grey neck by a narrow white stripe. Rump and upper and undertail coverts white, wings and rest of body slate-grey above, paler grey below. Non-breeding plumage: similar but head is pale grey, has dark patches around eyes and on ear coverts. Juveniles and immatures generally browner, have some mottling. Bill colour changes progressively from very dark brown and reddish at base to orange of adult.

Distribution & Habitat • Population estimated at a maximum of 5000 breeding pairs in the early 1980s. Has almost certainly decreased since and may now be threatened. Migratory within New Zealand. December–March after breeding most move from inland South Island breeding grounds to the coast, particularly to rivermouths, estuaries, harbours and lagoons. The majority remain on the east coast of the South Island, but a small proportion regularly cross Cook Strait and can be found along Wellington, Hawke Bay and Bay of Plenty coasts. Bay of Plenty is the northernmost known regular wintering ground, very rarely recorded on the North Island west coast north of the Manawatu Estuary.

Behaviour & Food • During the breeding season usually feeds from fast-flowing rivers, nearby farmland and also at lakes, tarns, farm dams and recently ploughed or irrigated paddocks. During winter commonly feeds alone at sea not far offshore, also in groups over the lower reaches of rivers, coastal fields, lagoons and some oxidation ponds.

Feeds mainly on small fish, a wide variety of insects particularly beetles, earthworms and grass grub larvae. Frequently roosts with and near White-fronted Terns and/or Black-billed Gulls.

Breeding • Nests October–February in small colonies, often near nesting Black-billed Gulls. Found mainly well inland on gravel riverbeds in the eastern South Island. Nest sites susceptible to flooding, human disturbance, stock trampling, mammalian predation and invasion by introduced plants.

Top:
Juvenile Black-fronted Tern.

Above:
Adult Black-fronted Terns.

47

Caspian Tern/Taranui
Sterna caspia

Relatively common
native
Family: LARIDAE

Identification • Length 51 cm, weight 700 g. Largest tern in New Zealand. Size and large bright red bill make it easy to identify. Breeding plumage: forehead cap nape black, pale grey upperparts, white underparts and underwings dark at tips. Short, slightly forked tail, very short legs and feet black. Non-breeding plumage: cap heavily flecked with white, may be almost white. Immature is similar to non-breeding adult, bill progressively reddens, legs progressively darken with age.

Distribution & Habitat • New Zealand population probably less than 3500. Primarily inhabits shallow coastal waters, most commonly frequenting coastlines, harbours, estuaries, lakes and lower reaches of rivers. Seldom seen far inland. Some populations move varying distances after breeding, for example the autumn influx into such localities as Manukau Harbour and the Firth of Thames, and the northward move-ment of birds from the Invercargill colony.

Behaviour & Food • Flies with steady, shallow wingbeats, less buoyant than most terns but unmistakeably tern-like. Has harsh, frequent, grating cry, loudly emitted, particularly in flight. Usually a solitary feeder, close inshore on coasts or in rivermouths, feeds mainly on surface-swimming fish. Hunts in a characteristic manner: flies a few metres above the water, points bill downward, sights prey, hovers briefly then plunges steeply in.

Breeding • Mainly a coastal nester, September–January, on both main islands. Majority of birds are in long-established colonies on exposed shellbanks and sandbanks immediately above high-tide level. Some nest inland, for example as isolated pairs on South Island shingle riverbeds in association with colonies of Black-backed Gulls. Many colonies subject to mammalian predation and human disturbance.

Caspian Tern in flight.

Juvenile Caspian Tern (right) begging from adult.

48

White-fronted Tern/Tara
Sterna striata

Common native
Family: LARIDAE

Identification · Length 40 cm, weight 160 g. Medium-sized, graceful, black and white tern. Breeding plumage: jet-black crown and nape with narrow white forehead. White lores, pale grey upperparts and white underparts. Many have a conspicuous pinkish tinge on breasts, long outer tail streamers. Non-breeding plumage: cap recedes to above eyes, broader white forehead and mid-crown mottled. Immatures are like non-breeding adults. Juveniles are distinctive with their crown streaked black, white and buff, upperparts barred and mottled ash-grey. Bill black with a very pale tip, very short legs and feet black or reddish-black irrespective of age and season.

Distribution & Habitat · By far the most common tern. Often found in large flocks on New Zealand coast and is rarely seen inland. Population was estimated at 100,000 breeding pairs in the early 1980s, evidence indicates this number has since declined. Little is known about distribution in New Zealand at any particular time of year. After breeding a considerable number of young and some adults migrate to the southeastern Australian coast.

Behaviour & Food · Buoyant, graceful on the wing. Feeds almost exclusively in coastal waters, sometimes at the mouths of tidal creeks and on rivers. Frequently flocks above shoaling fish not far offshore, sometimes with other species. Flies into the wind, darts down and picks up its prey. Feeds mainly on small surface-shoaling fish. Catch sometimes stolen by skuas.

Breeding · Nests October–February, mostly on coast throughout New Zealand. Mainly found in larger colonies of various sizes on sandy beaches, shinglebanks and shellbanks. Smaller numbers nest on shores of coastal lakes, offshore rock-stacks, islands, coastal cliffs, often with or near other species, principally Red-billed Gulls, Black-billed Gulls and Caspian Terns. Nest sites are vulnerable to storm destruction, human interference, mammalian predation and encroachment of introduced plants.

Adult White-fronted Tern.

Juvenile White-fronted Tern.

49

Crested Tern
Sterna bergii

Rare tropical vagrant
Family: LARIDAE

Identification · Length 47 cm, weight 350 g. Large tern. Breeding plumage: white forehead, black crown and nape often erected as crest. Upperparts slaty-grey, underparts white. Non-breeding: crown white or streaked black. Immatures similar to non-breeding adults. Very short legs and feet blackish. Bill is long, slender and yellow with a greenish tinge.

Distribution & Habitat · Single adults in breeding or non-breeding plumage and immatures are occasionally seen in coastal areas, mostly in the North Island. Some may remain in one locality for years.

Behaviour & Food · Graceful in flight with a long sweeping action of wings. Often roosts with White-fronted Terns, conspicuous among them because of its larger size and yellowish bill. Feeds almost entirely on smaller marine fish obtained by diving.

Breeding · Nests widely including in Australia and on many islands of the tropical South Pacific.

Adult Crested Tern.

Crested Tern with deformed bill.

50

New Zealand Kingfisher/Kotare
Halcyon sancta vagans

Common native
Family: ALCEDINIDAE

Identification • Length 24 cm, weight 65 g. Small kingfisher. Male is more brightly coloured than the female with bright greenish-blue upperparts, underparts off-white to russety. Has a black stripe from the eye and a white collar that both extend around the back of the neck, separating the head from the rest of the upperparts. Immature is duller, has brownish mottling on its breast and the upperparts have buff feather edges. Has a large, pointed black bill and very short dark legs.

Distribution & Habitat • Widespread, common throughout most of New Zealand. Especially visible in coastal districts and lowlands during winter. Lives in a wide variety of habitats including tidal estuaries, rocky coastlines, mangrove swamps, freshwater wetlands including river and stream edges, developed farmland with scattered trees, native and exotic forest and suburban parks. Many move to coastal areas during winter.

Behaviour & Food • Usually solitary or in pairs but during winter several can be seen feeding in a small area of mudflat or over a short distance on tidal rocks. Hunts food from elevated positions such as powerlines, trees, driftwood, posts and rocks. Flies swiftly and directly and has a distinctive loud penetrating call. Feeds on a wide variety of prey including large insects, crabs, small fish, freshwater crayfish, tadpoles, lizards, earthworms, mice and even small birds.

Breeding • Nests October–February in a chamber at the end of a short tunnel in such places as standing rotten tree trunks, wounds in living trees, knotholes, clay banks by farm tracks, riverbanks and roadside cuttings.

Glossary

adult   a bird that has reached its fullest development.

breeding plumage   the plumage worn by a bird during the nesting period.

endemic New Zealand bird   a species whose natural breeding range is in New Zealand and nowhere else.

eye-ring or eyelid   the bare skin around a bird's eye.

immature   stage of plumage between the first moult and full breeding plumage (= subadult).

introduced New Zealand bird   a species that has been brought to New Zealand by people.

iris   the thin tissue in front of the lens of the eye.

juvenile   birds in their first plumage after replacing natal down.

migrant   a species that moves annually and seasonally between breeding and non-breeding areas.

native New Zealand bird   a species that is naturally found in New Zealand, including recently self-introduced species.

non-breeding plumage   the plumage worn by a bird outside the nesting period.

phase   a regularly occurring colour variant.

secondary feathers   the flight feathers of the inner wing.

speculum   iridescent patch on the upperside of secondary feathers of ducks.

superciliary streak or stripe   a marking above the eye of a bird.

vagrant   a species that occurs in a given area very infrequently, and whose normal range is in another area.

wattles   colourful fleshy drupes on either side of the gape.

Index of common and Maori names

Index of scientific names